LAST STOP, LONESOME TOWN

LAST STOP, LONESOME TOWN

TARA AZZOPARDI

Mansfield Press

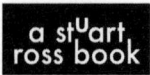

Copyright © Tara Azzopardi 2015
All rights reserved
Printed in Canada

Library and Archives Canada Cataloguing in Publication

Azzopardi, Tara, author
    Last stop, lonesome town / Tara Azzopardi.

Poems.
ISBN 978-1-77126-101-2 (paperback)

    I. Title.

PS8551.Z96L38 2015   C811'.54   C2015-906198-9

Editor: Stuart Ross
Typesetting & cover design: Stuart Ross
Cover photo: Christopher McDermott

The publication of *Last Stop, Lonesome Town* has been generously supported by the Canada Council for the Arts and the Ontario Arts Council.

Mansfield Press Inc.
25 Mansfield Avenue, Toronto, Ontario, Canada M6J 2A9
Publisher: Denis De Klerck
www.mansfieldpress.net

*To the memory of my father, David,
who introduced me to Ricky Nelson,
the song "Lonesome Town"
and a vast array of beautiful music*

CONTENTS

At the Party / 9
Teotihuacan / 10
The Vacation / 11
Agatha Christie, at Giza / 12
The Enemy's Moustache / 13
Brazil, 1908 / 14
A New Play by Ira Levin / 15
Modern Feminism / 18
Black Sabbath / 19
A Date with Casper / 20
Highway of Tears / 23
October 1939 / 24
City Council Meeting / 25
The Cult of Wasp / 26
Manifesto of the Penny Arcade / 27
Memo / 28
July / 29
Fort McMurray, Alberta / 30
Psychic Mysteries of Canada: Case #332 / 31
Nativity Play / 32
Love Poem for Christopher / 33
Bermuda Triangle / 34
The Great Depression / 36
Summertime, Ontario / 37
Lou Gehrig / 39
Shopping for a Suit / 40
I Keep Dreaming, Sam Cooke / 42
City Council Budget Meeting / 43
Albania, 1925 / 44
Industrial Evolution / 45

Bedlam, 9 a.m. / 46
The Band Plays On / 47
Nashville Rules / 49
Love Poem for Christopher II / 50
The Tenant / 51
The Bachelor / 52
Sex Club / 53
Helsinki / 54
Psychic Mysteries of Canada: Case #437 / 55
The Lady Vanishes / 56
No More Drama / 58
We Won't Stop Here / 59
What the Shadow Knows / 61
Alcatraz, 1962 / 62
The Ballad of Zerelda James / 64
Sun-up, Showdown / 68
The Bride Wore Sepia / 69
The Party / 70
Witness of the Penny Arcade / 71
Last Stop, Lonesome Town / 72
Bury My Body in New Orleans / 74

AT THE PARTY

There will be piñatas, shrimp with their tails,
baked Alaskas, a cake in the shape of a cloud.

We will talk about Freud, pyramids
and the Green Lantern.

Phyllis Diller will tell dirty jokes.
Vincent Price will teach French.

We'll play the zombie game, strip poker
and True Detective in the bedroom.

We'll have a dog show, a dance-off,
a beauty contest for Siamese twins.

A Swedish model will crawl on the floor, growling.

We'll dance to Joy Division and Neil Diamond
till three in the morning.

It will be the party
we'll never forget,
the party we'll never remember.

TEOTIHUACAN

We walk through the Avenue of the Dead
our sunscreen leaves streaks of white
ceremonial paint
cameras jingle like talismans
all the tourists and their fanny packs
climb the steps
of the Pyramid of the Sun
gulping water from plastic bottles
sweating over altars
of astrology and murder.

THE VACATION

We packed our bags in a hurry
left a note for the armadillo
the tarantula, the baby

our flight was delayed
for 23 days
we ate peanuts and bath salts
the Hindus prayed on the plane
the flight attendants
folded origami barf bags

our guide ushered us through the Andes
it was tedious and exhausting
and the crisp mountain air
paralyzed our smoggy, city lungs

while our son played video games
our daughter was sold to slavers

night crept into our hotel room
like a herd of angry cockroaches

we retched fast food, fast
as the tour bus whisked away
our notions of vacation
birds rained heavy on our heads
and the monkeys pelted us
with contempt.

AGATHA CHRISTIE, AT GIZA

Her mother tells her to
unfold her umbrella
she wishes she was married
the camels are winking
prisms through their tears
Agatha stares at the sun
standing in shadows, at Giza
she understands a mystery
and clutches it tight
between nervous thighs
and two sweaty palms.

THE ENEMY'S MOUSTACHE

The enemy's moustache is dark and foreboding,
we fear he trims it daily.
The enemy's moustache is cruel and unrelenting,
it harbours camels, sand and a time machine.
The enemy's moustache cannot be trusted,
our leaders have mouths we can plainly see.
The enemy's moustache is a menacing black cloud,
it rains down upon us, and interrupts
our regularly scheduled programming.

BRAZIL, 1908

My dearest Louisa,
the fever has worsened,
and the jungle grows by the minute.

The Indians have dug a trench
that spirals deep into my tent.

I am close to the Lost City.
The mediums in New York
are whispering the news:
Atlantis is buried here,
in a swamp of worms and broken tiles
lying in ruins
as I am, ruined.

A NEW PLAY BY IRA LEVIN

Act I

A man enters stage fright
the curtains draw upon
a woman giving birth to a mirror
the closet door swings open
and the ocean pours onto the audience

Act II

A girl aged seven
is visiting the zoo
she points to a boa constrictor
and shouts:
"Look, Mommy, New York!"

Act III

The bellhop
is good-looking, with auburn hair
and pale skin
his lips are like rosebuds
he loads the suitcases into the elevator
and closing the door
presses the tenth floor
his nails grow into grey talons

Act IV

Nuns huddle around the middle ages

INTERMISSION

Act V

A men's rights group
marches through the suburbs
banging drums
wearing capes
they want to cry in public
and can't

Act VI

Walt Disney sits at a table
he uses a knife
to adjust the robot

Act VII

A beautiful young woman
wearing a navy bikini
walks onstage
carrying a suitcase
she sets it on the floor
and opens it
green smoke spills out
and the audience is paralyzed
she puts on a ribbon
with the word *Hollywood*
and walks across the stage
waving

MODERN FEMINISM

Geraldine is photocopying a pamphlet
women who look like men
stand guard in black leather vests
the food is organized on tables

there is no gender in the word *president*
but our leader is named Azealia
and she's only 23.

BLACK SABBATH

I was 13
the period bled
through the black
staining the seat
a bloody goat.

A DATE WITH CASPER

The fire sparked, shooting embers
we were born
ghost children of the suburbs
we hovered in basements
invisible to Others
frightening them all
until daylight painted us
transparent

but I recognized this behind
pools of black
another one
damaged by eight years old
united by Goth, Halloween
and being eternal
knowing adults are crazy
and life
is terribly wondrous

but mostly doomed

we were born to die
and we sat in the mall parking lot
laughing

we made our club
at the shack in the woods
drawing blood
bodies pressed together
tracing pentagrams in the dirt

as teenagers
our hair became
tangled masks
and old ladies
gasped at the sight of us
pock-faced creatures scowling
blowing smoke
into crowded bus shelters

ripped jeans, old radios
swigging whisky, then beer
cutting 666 skulls into our arms
thrashing under a bridge
barfing in the river
watching it elope with the muddy current

crumpled paper bags, condoms, cigarettes on concrete
silky layers of grease
and the smell of lighter fluid everywhere

we slept in a pile, shivering thin
leather jackets in morning rain
feral dogs, clutching madly
exhausted from
running wild with emotion.

it'd be a miracle if we reached 20

exorcised by family
ourselves

living in a car
and surrounded by salt
the plastic bags
roll around like tumbleweeds

and the tapes keep playing
down in a hole, shout at the devil
never mind, so

let's say goodnight to the world
the witches will tuck us in.

HIGHWAY OF TEARS

Mountains vanish
into the ocean
driving down the highway
to Vancouver
we throw trash
out the windows
brown stains
coffee cups
balled-up underwear
like snakes coiled in the ditch

Angela is smoking
and talking about her baby
inhaling heavy
we take the pipe
and throw it at asphalt
dead animals
rotting at noon
I look at their little claws

angry men in trucks
we throw trash out the windows
eating chips and pepperoni sticks
lunch before we're lost
in the city

killing on the road
sometimes it looks just like meat
dead animals
wishing for another chance

OCTOBER 1939

Children wear Halloween masks
dogs tilt their heads, understanding

CITY COUNCIL MEETING

Being a bylaw to amend a bylaw
being a bylaw to amend a
bylaw being a bylaw
to amend a bylaw
being a bylaw to amend
a being

THE CULT OF WASP

We have quietly determined you will live here
etched into magnificence
swirling in brick and asphalt
spirals
a maple tree here
a boxwood bush there.

And please, everyone
maintain your distance
with sharply edged lawns
block your neighbour's view
park your large vehicles
in front of your house

talk only if you need to
when the power lines
go down for half an hour
stay tight-lipped
and apologize if you drink
too much
in your backyard
on the 1st of July.

Never fart or if we do
they are always cold and silent.

MANIFESTO OF THE PENNY ARCADE

Resurrect the imagination. Infect it.
Cure conservatism with quinine and opium.
Infest the protoplasm. Teach hydrogen.
Embrace your doppelgänger. Waltz the danse macabre.
Annihilate the upper class. Replace it with clairvoyant lobsters.
Congregate and sigh in séances.
Conjure the ghost of Lili Marlene. Elect her as mayor.
Spike the water supply with sonnets.
Rhyme in rhapsody. Foresee futurists.
Pray for the plague of Joan of Arc.
Redefine hedonism in Glaswegian fashion.
Preach perversity. Repeat in sincerity.
Go out with a bang so they don't forget you.
Denounce apathy. Scream with the banshees.
Love with the intensity of a silent film star. Taint the mainstream.
Sleepwalk through the swamps.
Translate the song of swallows.
Regurgitate a saint. Begin again.

MEMO

At 2:33 p.m., we will stand
at the water cooler
and stare into nothing.

JULY

The guys at Chubby Burger
whistle at her
bouncing ponytail
and factory-shredded micro-shorts
she's snapping her gum, just 15
and rolling her eyes at them
guys digging at roads, in orange vests
rolling out the tar
guys with kids at home
watching her lope past them

everyone under the spell
of the promise of it
dogs are fucking in the driveway
she keeps going
but her gazelle legs
wave back at them

FORT McMURRAY, ALBERTA

The worker is grateful for this day:
for the shift he has just finished,
for his newfound ability
to withstand sulphur and burn.
He sees the foreman,
and is thankful for him, a good guy,
big and doughy with pellucid eyes.
The worker is thankful for his country's leader,
and for this great company
grinding oil from tar and sand:
spitting out a black, dense,
hovering cloud.

PSYCHIC MYSTERIES OF CANADA: CASE #332
BRANDON, MANITOBA

Mary Patterson witnesses
her uncooked Sunday ham
levitating

NATIVITY PLAY

Everyone is enjoying the nativity play
it smells like fir, candles
good feelings
we love children in costumes
and it is all warmly amusing until
the ass farts
and Joseph drops Jesus
knocking the holy spirit
clean out of him.

LOVE POEM FOR CHRISTOPHER

I would come to you
at dawn
when the wrens are fleeing the trees
and rabbits leap from heavy earth.
Even in the great storm:
a black eclipse,
wet skin on bone.
Even when the roads are littered with burdock
and snares,
I would come to you.
Even when the fruit rots
to the ground,
when the crop is bent with blight,
I will come to you.
I hold your hand to my breast
and we find shelter in the pines,
warmth in the hollow.

BERMUDA TRIANGLE

As a child
I wondered about it for hours
lost in a pyramid
I sank in quicksand
grabbing at roots
because jungle vines
lay limp and
always out of reach

and still
I was caught and pulled under
its magnetic depth
its unforgiving fog.
Broken planes
without wings
great coffins
rocking silent in the deep
ghost ships
drifted and mourned
echoing the last call
of the Loch Ness Monster
who died here, too
snarled in wreckage
of other dinosaurs
and fossils of
all great things.
The Yeti
drowned in the
broken palace of Atlantis
hairy and strewn

with seaweed
queen to Druids
eternally pushing stones
against the currents
of salt.

I'm still wondering
the hows and whys:
of Incans and Egyptians
aliens and magicians
voodoo and witches
of Easter Island
of Mayans
shrunken heads
the undead
and why it still
haunts me
why this pyramid
is a boxing ring
and it beat me with torrents
of what appeared to be love
when all I've ever wanted
was flight
and instead
I'm on the last
gasp of the *Titanic*.

THE GREAT DEPRESSION

With $1.50 left to our name
we entered her in
the beauty pageant
her pin curls wept out
sagging from the heat
she stood on the stage
and bled straight through her dress
bad luck continued
like a Louisiana hex
and the baby cried
Wah wah wah
wah wah wah wah.

SUMMERTIME, ONTARIO

We run around the block
throw balls against garage doors
in alleys
where cats spray
and raccoons eat their buffets
our running shoes will be ruined
by the end of summer

the air smells like hamburgers
gasoline and sun-baked concrete
when the knife-sharpening guy
turns the corner
ringing a bell
we grab our guns and run for cover

waiting for the mail to come
laughing at teenagers and their greasy jobs
their greasy-angry faces
wishing I was Spiderman for the 800th time

the detective agency is open for business
we make cards and promise
to find lost dogs
wallets and glasses

on Sundays
everyone is angry until we go to the lake
and for a while Dad teases
and Mom laughs at his jokes
for a while my brother spends time

reading comics with me
our dog is exhausted from swimming
I'm not so fat from swimming
we enjoy being away from our lives

I think about sex constantly
it's abstract and alluring:
I want to make it with a vampire

can we get ice cream
and spy on the Nazi
who lives on the corner?

LOU GEHRIG

Why is that name
so horrible
when all you
wanted to do
was play baseball?

SHOPPING FOR A SUIT

I am surprised at the cost of men's suits
"Jingle Bells" is on the intercom

the menswear department is a sea of stacks
shirts are squared off into plastic packs
suits hang from a circular rack
huddling together: black, navy, brown
the ties are bright, almost gaudy.
I have my father's old suit in a plastic bag
the one he wore before the sickness
and now I am searching for a size
his body has never known before
everything looks too big.
We are enormous, bulky with bread and health
he is shrivelled down to the crooked body
in the living room
that we turn, turn, turn.
I'm confused by the shirts
they fall out of my hands like playing cards
where there are checks
I see the tarot skull, death
this tie is too cheery
this suit doesn't match the casket
this shirt costs $89
seems criminal to buy it
then bury it

How many other shoppers
are buying clothes for a funeral?
someone in the shoe department

buying pumps for her mother
no one sees the feet of the dead,
but the shoes must match
flowers in December, when nothing grows
the perfume department reeks
my headache grows from the scent
of fake lilies and roses

I keep thinking of tiny Asian women
sewing furiously with tiny hands
making suits overseas
folding shirts into plastic
and me with my mom's credit card
buying my dad his funeral suit

the intercom is playing
"I'll Be home for Christmas"
this must be a bad dream

I keep the paper receipt
long after he dies,
remembering.

I KEEP DREAMING, SAM COOKE

for David Azzopardi

A cabin leans tall
against the afternoon sun,
wallpapered with Hollywood stories,
astrology forecasts
and the news of 1958.

There are biscuits in the pan
and fresh coffee on the stove.
Bees swimming in clover,
it smells like summertime.
There are no tragedies,
until the day reaches its end
and I keep dreaming Sam Cooke.

I keep dreaming, Sam Cooke.

CITY COUNCIL BUDGET MEETING

Gasoline
Car shows
Summer Olympics in Ontario
Discretion benefits
Goose control program
Homelessness
People with dementia

ALBANIA, 1925

We left Albania in 1925.
My mother packed a brooch, a cocker spaniel
and a jar of pickled eggs.
My father shaved his body hair
and tied newspaper to his legs.
On the ocean, he drank kerosene and perfume.
My mother gave birth to asthmatic twins
who wheezed a concerto at night.

The journey lasted 52 days.
The twins nursed on pickled eggs.
We landed in Montreal and worked till dusk in a laundromat.

We bought a shop for the brooch
and sold eye patches for 12¢ apiece.

When I grew taller than everyone
Albania became a memory,
a postcard,
an outdated part
in our modern-parted hair.

THE INDUSTRIAL EVOLUTION

There was a machine that _____
people used to make the machine
people used to make parts of the machine
sometimes people used other machines
to make this machine
now there is a different machine
a more improved machine
it requires fewer people
to make the improved machine
sometimes the parts break
sometimes the machine becomes redundant.

Sometimes people keep the redundant machines
in museums
where they are functional, but still redundant
and sometimes a few people are employed
in the museums
that house the old machines
where other people can visit
the redundant machines
and talk about the past
and how life was better, but worse.

BEDLAM, 9 A.M.

Waking wide, a haze of white
bandaged ear to ear
Peter Lorre as the Doctor
grinning, whispering
"Operation. Operation."

THE BAND PLAYS ON

The clarinets squeal
the musicians are drunk

Mimi Van Boren is bored
wearing her cloak of moths
she complains there's soup in her hair

crickets crawl out of the biscuits
the cakes are hard as plastic
the roast beef swims
in a pool of blood

no one cares about the trenches

the waiters hate jazz
they tap-dance across the floor
spilling food on velvet dresses

Count Ferdinand Von Zeppelin
eats a plate of mashed potatoes
leaves his beard on the table
and waltzes with his hernia
dripping cola on Vienna

the volcano spits children and snakes
the bartenders spray seltzer on everyone
Jack Benny's had enough
the parrots are pissed
the Russians want an apology

the Mole mutters in a corner
sing low, sweet Harriet

Casey falls on a strawberry blonde
crushing the dreams of King Kong
the lawyers are called
everyone demands a refund

and the band plays on.

NASHVILLE RULES

When the country singer
arrives at the studio
please ensure there is
cough syrup in her cup

when the country singer
sits in her leather chair
please ensure the audience
is blinded by the sequins
on her shirt

when the country singer
croons her hit song
please ensure the coyotes
howl in key

when the country singer
chooses to answer a question
please ensure your ears
are dumbed with rags and
honeycomb

when the country singer
decides to leave
please ensure she is
lowered through the floor
and the audience is weeping
hearts of leather and suede.

LOVE POEM FOR CHRISTOPHER II

I keep thinking
about what it's like
to make coffee with you
in the morning
with the smell of bacon frying
and wet dogs
all around us.
I wanted independence
like the union rep
in a tie and jean jacket.
It's nice to read the paper to you.
The community never looked better.

THE TENANT

He only plays Chopin
the music waltzes down the hall
a brown liquid
seeps out from apartment 366
when I knock at the door
I ask about the carpet
are you alright
something brushes against my elbow

when the door opens
I'm standing in a room
ankles mired in fondue
Boris will take your coat, they say
I have nothing to give
but my eternal company.

THE BACHELOR

Everyone wants to date the doctor
he's the most eligible bachelor in town
he wears gloves made from Italian eels
he speaks 56 languages
and plays viola with
the mercury-poisoned opera
he wears Algerian dust jackets
and bows to shadows in the night
he can cook rice
and smokes cigarettes
rolled by Lebanese merchants
he can tango with an ostrich
gamble with an alligator.

Everyone wants to date the doctor
in a lampshade
in a dumb-waiter
at a grand ball and
in the orchestra
a sports car
a hot-air balloon
an escalator.

He snakes fast between gender
oh the snark has sharp teeth
and he will sink them deep.

SEX CLUB

On the 3rd floor
they're eating doughnuts
poking their tongues
through holes
squeezing out jelly
the couches are sticky

the hot tub
is insecure

in the Roman room
people lie on the floor
waiting for a woman
to shit grapes
into their mouths

no one will wander
into the red room
it is haunted by Santa
bellowing his phony
oh oh ohs

in the dungeon
in the basement
they're whipping
bags of Jell-O
and white people in chains
are calling themselves slaves.

HELSINKI

I don't know what to think
everyone is mute until they are drinking
everyone is cold
until they are drinking
the woods are burning
and the light is blinding
everyone albino.

PSYCHIC MYSTERIES OF CANADA: CASE #437
PERTH, NEW BRUNSWICK

After her house is struck by lightning,
Sheila Harvey's head trembles slightly
before the toast starts to burn
she can always predict a rainfall
her cat does nothing but hiss at her

THE LADY VANISHES

I'm watching him flirt, casually.

From a cool Scandinavian height
he sends her a smile
painting the room golden
in just an instant

everyone notices.

I am dark and burning down,
a thousand islands
consumed by fiery volcanoes
fill my veins and turn me into
a pile of hot ash
in the corner of the bar

it is a murder, of sorts.

He blinks, brushes aside
his flaxen, pony hair
quietly making a joke

and her laugh
shatters all the
mirrors of Edmonton.

The sound is deafening
the dumpy kid with the overbite
wears ill-fitting, second-hand clothes
smelling like soup
like musty basements, like the old girlfriend.

While they whisper like conspirators
I'm the sweaty brunette:
the sad secretary, overlooked
and desperate to chip away
the impenetrable,
blond ice.

NO MORE DRAMA

I can't assume anything
and I'm trying not to judge

my ex is one step away
from hiring a Filipino nanny
and one step closer to
practicing Scientology

his new wife takes pictures
of quinoa salads
moulded in the shape of a heart

and I'm getting my hair pulled
in dirty basements
fucking without condoms
or care.

WE WON'T STOP HERE

for R. Brautigan

Hunger makes the rocks
rumble in my shirt pocket
going back to Oregon
sand along the train tracks
I'm dragging my feet
through a hangover

my hat is an apple
that falls to the ground
and bruises my ego

Marion, Sharon, Leanne:
forgive my bad breath
forgive my bad head

Virginia, Akiko, Marcia, Janice:
only so much
can be blamed on my mother

Ianthe is the daughter
of mythology
she weaves her webs
with finesse
the child can conquer the Civil War

but can't we drive
to San Francisco
I hear they pay the poets there

I need a new jacket
it's had enough of my arms' depression
it wants a divorce
the letters arrive daily

the goldfish in the toilet bowl
are swimming in circles

I stare out to the ocean
I need the general
to salute my moustache
I need to fold my head
into the broken floor

WHAT THE SHADOW KNOWS

Morocco is for the lonely and romantic.
The children love a Western star named Slappy Millshanks.
Monkeys know more than you think.
Japanese supermodels shoot ice from their eyes.
Peter Lorre loved backgammon and hashish.
Psychics solve murders on the can.
Porgy didn't love Bess.
Russian boys make the best sailors.
Octopi cure hangovers upon request.
Gary Cooper talked to horses.
Orchids bloom on tears and milk.
The Revolution will begin with a Mexican named Lupe.
When you leave the room, the animals discuss you at length.

ALCATRAZ, 1962

The guy with hepatitis
shaking in the bunk below
says the city is changing

the carpet of fog
and the neon signs
are going out of fashion
it's all sunshine
and girls in short-shorts
blondes for every boy

I stare out across the water
hear the city purring
hookers with halos of hair
cars honking at junkies
weaving around the streets
Jesus preachers and
Chinese gamblers
everybody
at the edge of America

chop suey in a diner
followed by black coffee
a couple of bucks
for beer and a party
a girl in the back seat
a stolen car
gasping at salt air
heaving in an alley

the thief beside me
grumbles
it's all a lie
that city is just
a shithole like the rest
cops on every corner
and crooked faggots
with wormy fingers
behind every door

I'd still take San Quentin
over this
perched atop a rock
a goose-necked coward
surrounded by rapists
white-trash murderers
everyone honing a blade
to stick you deep in the ribs

anything's better
than staring at
San Francisco
blinding bright on a Sunday afternoon

THE BALLAD OF ZERELDA JAMES

A line of smoke
rises grey and tall from the hill
it tells me
he is near, or dead
or both.

Even in dry heat
wretched summer
children filthy
and squealing like
pigs in the muck
wasps crawling over apple-rot
flies glued to butter
I am waiting.
Or worse:
winter bleaching the countryside
grey-ash and anemic
fingers blue
washing wool in ice water
rinsing dirt in dirty water
waiting
for his black shadow
to return.

I know when he's close.

The hairs on my neck reach up
I drop the dishes
and sing silly tunes

wearing my best dress
until it's stained
and smelling like onions
the horses whinny
running circles in the pen
and he fills up the doorway
blocking all light from the room.

A flock of doves
take flight in my breast.

His beard is dark
as the devil's pet
I have stroked it, lovingly
while he slumbers deep
and I am finally content
wanting only to lie beside him entwined
in our own sad malevolence
the floor a river of fire
honeymooning on Lucifer's raft.

One minute he is kicking the dog
and the next
he is cradling it in his arms
caressing its ears
its soft brown head.

He has murdered six men
just as I have murdered
the very thought of their kin

wives and mothers
babies, erased clean
crumbs brushed off a table.

A neglected child from birth
he rages against the Union
and all those in vest-coats
clean leather boots
an angry boy-teen
smothered in the arms
of exhausted Mother Confederacy
young punk rutting
in a swamp of defeat.

Drinking in the night
whisky, moonshine
jugs of forgetting
and remembering
faded glory
faces blown to shards
of bone and blood.

Surrounded by the skittish:
eternally boys, legally men
they sleep on pallets on the floor
nip at each other
nervously await his bark
dream of holding a gun
to his head
and ending this sickness.

When the bullet shatters his skull
and he crumples to a heap
bleeding onto the linseed floor
we are released
into the November afternoon.

Sleep, at last.
Sleep.

SUN-UP, SHOWDOWN

We sat in the saloon for hours
maybe days
it could've been a dog's birthday
a sickly jury
a silver widow's anniversary.

Rain dripped from ceiling
to floor
we sat, silent
inhaling sawdust, downing whisky
piano keys flickering
Matilda laughing.

A rooster crowed
a donkey coughed
a rattlesnake slid from your boot.

We argued, bone-tired
damning each other
a Job's life through.

Lady's luck lasted all of nine months
and gambling men had had their day:
a fortune in gold, handkerchief tucked neat
a desert, a cemetery
away.

THE BRIDE WORE SEPIA

She emerges from the sea in the morning
her face sunken deep under a veil
of fishing nets and seaweed dragging a trail of shells, bones

her bridesmaids skitter aside:
seagulls drape a worm-eaten dress over sand
crabs scatter pebbles like confetti
her blue fingers grasp a skeletal collection of driftwood.

The circle opens to
the sailor lost at sea
pale and shivering in his rotted vest
hopeful in the early light, out of the depths
awaiting his bride
and a honeymoon in the undertow.

THE PARTY

for M. Connery

We are preparing for the party
oysters are being served
by miniature ponies
and rhesus monkeys
are serving miniature pony.

Everyone has tails.

The children are practicing their act:
A Brief History of the Black Plague
in 44 Tableaus.

Mother sets the table
with tortoise shells and false nails
Father decorates the hallway
with bouquets of Band-Aids on Jell-O

I'm practicing my speech
for the deaf on the deaf by the deaf.

The Pomeranian is panting on the couch
and the servants fan him
with ostrich plumes
rolling their eyes.

WITNESS OF THE PENNY ARCADE

I saw the straw break the camel's back
I heard the doves mourn their song
I saw the bibliographer of Bedlam
I saw the saints suffer from syphilis
I saw Victorians invent the Ouija board
I saw a couple neck in the neck of the woods
I saw Tom Dooley hang from a white oak tree
I saw the manatees sleep
I saw Lazarus drink the cup of hemlock
I saw a witch drowned in Salem
I saw the revolution, and the Fenians won
I saw Prometheus, Frankenstein and the Golem play checkers
       in a laundromat
I saw a Coney Island monkey living in a box
I saw Siamese twins sue each other
I saw a poodle attack a pit bull
I heard a honky-tonk jukebox spill the ghost of Hank Williams
I saw a pear embalmed in a jar
I saw Mata Hari smoke the hookah
I saw a Jacobean murder a Walmart
I saw a Berliner lose her eyelash, crying in a cabaret
I saw punks pass out in the Chelsea Hotel
I saw the ocean dream a final undertow
I saw my bones bobbing in the soup pot
I saw the marrow go soft.

LAST STOP, LONESOME TOWN

By Grand Central Station
I sat down, got wasted
Junior beside me
muttering Appalachian
wiping snot with toilet paper
my ticket is a fortune cookie
it shatters in my pocket
in the maze of memory, forgetting
I lose the luggage, the language
the history books
the I Ching of "what ifs"
I shuffle around in second-hand shoes
with a stale ham sandwich
in a brown paper bag.

Hustled on the train
by a bunch of ruthless orphans
I reach into my pocket
and the badger bites my finger
the porter demands a ticket
we give him a sob story
the woe-is-me's,
together, alone
a pack of bloodhounds
howling in the boxcar
don't cry for me, concertina
Junior is
anemic and leaking whisky
his feet are longer than I thought

in the corner
children are reading Gogol
learning about Russian childhoods
peering out the window
feeling Ontario
looking like Ohio
the last of the wastelands
wash up on Great Lake shores
the train winds around a hangover
everything is dirty
my heart wanted purity

as we pull out of the station
a line of exes wave adieu
but this goodbye is final

we begin humming "Lili Marlene"
we no longer cage animals
we break for the heartbroken
the conductor calls out our destination
our journey is the last stop
we wipe the tears from our eyes with ghosts.

BURY MY BODY IN NEW ORLEANS

When the flood hits
and the hurricane
rains asphalt and shopping carts
and the parade is broken
foam and everything
is swimming in shredded plastic
wrap it in a shower curtain
dig that grave deep
and I will be queen
of the dirty swamp
of the dead done cheap

ACKNOWLEDGEMENTS

Some of these poems have appeared, sometimes in an earlier form, in *Perpetual Motion Machine*, issues 1, 2, and 3; *Surreal Estate: 13 Canadian Poets Under the Influence* (The Mercury Press, 2004); *Rogue Stimulus: The Stephen Harper Holiday Anthology for a Prorogued Parliament* (Mansfield Press, 2011); *The Week Shall Inherit the Verse* (online).

I'd like to express my extreme gratitude and appreciation to my mother, Linda Azzopardi, and brother, Jason Azzopardi, for their infinite love and support. To Mark Connery, Beverly Taft, Michael Comeau, and Sonja Ahlers for inspiration, encouragement, and being stellar friends. To Christopher McDermott, for helping me see what I couldn't see, for so long.

To Denis De Klerck and Mansfield Press for having faith in this strange work. And to Stuart Ross, my editor and long-time friend: thank you for always believing in me as a writer, for your thoughtful advice, generous guidance, and persistent encouragement. Without you, none of this would've been possible.

Tara Azzopardi grew up in Etobicoke, Ontario. She has worked as a clerk in a costume shop, a walking courier, a contract archaeologist, a property manager, an independent video store clerk, an organic farmer, as well as in construction and as a historical interpreter in a pioneer village. She currently lives in eastern Ontario and occasionally makes art and music there. *Last Stop, Lonesome Town* is her first book of poetry.

OTHER BOOKS FROM MANSFIELD PRESS

Poetry

Leanne Averbach, *Fever*
Nelson Ball, *In This Thin Rain*
Nelson Ball, *Some Mornings*
Gary Barwin, *Moon Baboon Canoe*
George Bowering, *Teeth: Poems 2006–2011*
Stephen Brockwell, *Complete Surprising Fragments of Improbable Books*
Stephen Brockwell & Stuart Ross, eds., *Rogue Stimulus: The Stephen Harper Holiday Anthology for a Prorogued Parliament*
Diana Fitzgerald Bryden, *Learning Russian*
Alice Burdick, *Flutter*
Alice Burdick, *Holler*
Jason Camlot, *What The World Said*
Margaret Christakos, *wipe.under.a.love*
Pino Coluccio, *First Comes Love*
Marie-Ève Comtois, *My Planet of Kites*
Dani Couture, *YAW*
Gary Michael Dault, *The Milk of Birds*
Frank Davey, *Poems Suitable to Current Material Conditions*
Pier Giorgio Di Cicco, *The Dark Time of Angels*
Pier Giorgio Di Cicco, *Dead Men of the Fifties*
Pier Giorgio Di Cicco, *The Honeymoon Wilderness*
Pier Giorgio Di Cicco, *Living in Paradise*
Pier Giorgio Di Cicco, *Early Works*
Pier Giorgio Di Cicco, *The Visible World*
Salvatore Difalco, *What Happens at Canals*
Christopher Doda, *Aesthetics Lesson*
Christopher Doda, *Among Ruins*
Glen Downie, *Monkey Soap*
Rishma Dunlop, *The Body of My Garden*
Rishma Dunlop, *Lover Through Departure: New and Selected Poems*
Rishma Dunlop, *Metropolis*
Rishma Dunlop & Priscila Uppal, eds., *Red Silk: An Anthology of South Asian Women Poets*
Ollivier Dyens, *The Profane Earth*
Laura Farina, *Some Talk of Being Human*
Jaime Forsythe, *Sympathy Loophole*
Carole Glasser Langille, *Late in a Slow Time*
Eva HD, *Rotten Perfect Mouth*
Suzanne Hancock, *Another Name for Bridge*
Jason Heroux, *Emergency Hallelujah*
Jason Heroux, *Memoirs of an Alias*
Jason Heroux, *Natural Capital*
John B. Lee, *In the Terrible Weather of Guns*
Jeanette Lynes, *The Aging Cheerleader's Alphabet*
David W. McFadden, *Abnormal Brain Sonnets*
David W. McFadden, *Be Calm, Honey*
David W. McFadden, *Shouting Your Name Down the Well: Tankas and Haiku*
David W. McFadden, *What's the Score?*
Kathryn Mockler, *The Purpose Pitch*
Leigh Nash, *Goodbye, Ukulele*
Lillian Necakov, *The Bone Broker*
Lillian Necakov, *Hooligans*
Peter Norman, *At the Gates of the Theme Park*
Peter Norman, *Water Damage*
Natasha Nuhanovic, *Stray Dog Embassy*
Catherine Owen & Joe Rosenblatt, with Karen Moe, *Dog*
Corrado Paina, *The Alphabet of the Traveler*
Corrado Paina, *Cinematic Taxi*
Corrado Paina, *The Dowry of Education*
Corrado Paina, *Hoarse Legend*
Corrado Paina, *Souls in Plain Clothes*
Nick Papaxanthos, *Love Me Tender*
Stuart Ross et al., *Our Days in Vaudeville*
Matt Santateresa, *A Beggar's Loom*
Matt Santateresa, *Icarus Redux*
Ann Shin, *The Last Thing Standing*
Jim Smith, *Back Off, Assassin! New and Selected Poems*
Jim Smith, *Happy Birthday, Nicanor Parra*
Robert Earl Stewart, *Campfire Radio Rhapsody*
Robert Earl Stewart, *Something Burned on the Southern Border*
Carey Toane, *The Crystal Palace*
Aaron Tucker, *Punchlines*
Priscila Uppal, *Sabotage*
Priscila Uppal, *Summer Sport: Poems*
Priscila Uppal, *Winter Sport: Poems*
Steve Venright, *Floors of Enduring Beauty*
Brian Wickers, *Stations of the Lost*

Fiction

Marianne Apostolides, *The Lucky Child*
Sarah Dearing, *The Art of Sufficient Conclusions*
Denis De Klerck, ed., *Particle & Wave: A Mansfield Omnibus of Electro-Magnetic Fiction*
Salvatore Difalco, *Mean Season*
Paula Eisenstein, *Flip Turn*
Sara Heinonen, *Dear Leaves, I Miss You All*
Christine Miscione, *Carafola*
Marko Sijan, *Mongrel*
Tom Walmsley, *Dog Eat Rat*
Corinne Wasilewski, *Live from the Underground*

Non-Fiction

George Bowering, *How I Wrote Certain of My Books*
Denis De Klerck & Corrado Paina, eds., *College Street–Little Italy: Toronto's Renaissance Strip*
Pier Giorgio Di Cicco, *Municipal Mind: Manifestos for the Creative City*
Amy Lavender Harris, *Imagining Toronto*
David W. McFadden, *Mother Died Last Summer*
Deborah Verginella, ed., *Bon Appetito Toronto!*

For a complete list of Mansfield Press titles, please visit mansfieldpress.net